Smart E-commerce

Tips for Building a Profitable Online Business

Basil U.

COPYRIGHT PAGE

All right reserved. No part of this publication may be published in any means or by any form, either by photocopying, scanning or otherwise without any prior written permission from the copyright holder.

Copyright © 2024 Basil U.

About the Author

Basil is a software engineer based in Dubai, United Arab Emirate, he has worked as a Developer for over 8 years and has been building dynamic web applications, for personal and for companies world wide.

In the time past his experience has helped different kinds of companies ranging from startups to large scale enterprises. He is also vast in knowledge with CLoud Computation, Mobile Application Development, AI Integration, API Integration and Databases.

I am grateful to my family who has been a huge support to me since I started writing this book. Thanks to my wife Onyi and children for their endless support.

Content

Introduction
Chapter One
Getting Started with E-commerce
Chapter Two
Finding a Profitable Niche
Chapter Three
Product Selection and Sourcing
Chapter Four
Building a Strong Brand
Chapter Five
Optimizing Your Online Store
Chapter Six
Marketing and Sales Strategies
Chapter Seven
Customer Acquisition and Retention
Chapter Eight
Analyzing and Improving Performance
Chapter Nine
Managing Finances and Scaling Up
Chapter Ten
Case Studies and Success Stories
Chapter Eleven
Conclusion

Introduction

What is E-commerce?

E-commerce, short for electronic commerce, refers to the buying and selling of goods and services over the internet. It encompasses a wide range of online business activities, including retail shopping, online banking, online auctions, and internet bill payment. Essentially, e-commerce is any commercial transaction conducted electronically through the internet.

E-commerce can be classified into several major types:

1. **Business-to-Consumer (B2C):** This is the most common form of e-commerce, where businesses sell products or services directly to consumers. Examples include online retailers like Amazon and Walmart.
2. **Business-to-Business (B2B):** In this model, businesses sell products or services to other businesses. This can include wholesale suppliers, manufacturers, and service providers.

3. **Consumer-to-Consumer (C2C):** This involves transactions between individual consumers, often facilitated by third-party platforms such as eBay, Craigslist, or Etsy.
4. **Consumer-to-Business (C2B):** In this less common model, individuals sell products or services to businesses. Examples include freelancers offering services to companies through platforms like Upwork.
5. **Business-to-Government (B2G) and Government-to-Business (G2B):** These involve transactions between businesses and government entities, such as procurement contracts and tax services.
6. **Mobile Commerce (M-commerce):** A subset of e-commerce that involves transactions conducted via mobile devices like smartphones and tablets.

The rise of e-commerce has been driven by several factors, including the widespread adoption of internet-connected devices, advances in technology, and changing consumer behaviors. It offers numerous advantages over traditional brick-and-mortar retail, such as convenience, a wider selection of products, and often lower prices.

Importance of Profitability in E-commerce

While the e-commerce landscape presents vast opportunities, achieving profitability in this highly competitive space is a significant challenge. Profitability is the cornerstone of any successful e-commerce business, ensuring its sustainability, growth, and long-term success. Here's why profitability is crucial in e-commerce:

1. **Sustainability and Growth:**
    - Profitability allows businesses to reinvest in their operations, enhancing infrastructure, expanding product lines, and improving customer service.
    - Sustainable profit margins enable companies to weather economic downturns and market fluctuations, ensuring long-term viability.

2. **Competitive Advantage:**
    - Profitable businesses can afford to invest in marketing, research and development, and technology, giving them an edge over less profitable competitors.
    - They can offer better pricing, promotions, and customer incentives without compromising their bottom line.
3. **Investor Confidence:**
    - Profitability attracts investors and can significantly enhance a company's ability to raise capital.
    - It signals financial health and management effectiveness, increasing investor trust and interest.
4. **Operational Efficiency:**
    - Focusing on profitability encourages businesses to streamline operations, reduce costs, and improve efficiency.

- Efficient operations lead to better inventory management, reduced waste, and optimized supply chains.

5. **Customer Trust and Loyalty:**
    - Profitable businesses can invest in quality products, customer service, and user experience, fostering customer satisfaction and loyalty.
    - Happy and loyal customers are more likely to make repeat purchases and recommend the business to others.

6. **Innovation and Adaptation:**
    - Financial stability enables businesses to innovate and adapt to changing market trends and consumer demands.
    - Profitability supports experimentation with new products, services, and business models.

Achieving profitability requires a strategic approach, including effective marketing, competitive pricing, cost management, and a deep understanding of the target market. Throughout this book, we will explore various strategies and tips to help you build a profitable e-commerce business.

Overview of What the Book Will Cover

This book is designed to provide you with practical and actionable tips to enhance the profitability of your e-commerce business. Whether you're a seasoned e-commerce entrepreneur or just starting, you'll find valuable insights and strategies to optimize your operations and boost your bottom line. Here's a brief overview of what each chapter will cover:

1. **Getting Started with E-commerce:**
    - We'll begin with the basics of setting up an online store, including choosing the right e-commerce platform, designing your website, and ensuring compliance with legal and financial regulations.
2. **Finding a Profitable Niche:**
    - Learn how to conduct market research, identify trends, and evaluate competition to

select a niche that offers high profitability potential.

3. **Product Selection and Sourcing:**
   - Discover the criteria for choosing profitable products and explore various sourcing options, from manufacturers to wholesalers and dropshipping. We'll also discuss effective inventory management practices.

4. **Building a Strong Brand:**
   - Understand the importance of branding and how to create a unique value proposition. We'll cover branding strategies that can set your business apart in a crowded market.

5. **Optimizing Your Online Store:**
   - Explore best practices for designing a user-friendly website, crafting compelling product descriptions, and optimizing for mobile devices to enhance the shopping experience.

6. **Marketing and Sales Strategies:**
    - Learn about different marketing channels, including SEO, PPC advertising, social media, and email marketing, and how to leverage them to drive traffic and sales.
7. **Customer Acquisition and Retention:**
    - Find out how to attract new customers and keep existing ones through excellent customer service, loyalty programs, and feedback loops.
8. **Analyzing and Improving Performance:**
    - Delve into key performance indicators (KPIs) for e-commerce, and discover tools and strategies for analyzing data and continuously improving your operations.
9. **Managing Finances and Scaling Up:**
    - Get practical tips on financial management, from budgeting to cash flow management, and learn strategies for scaling your business while maintaining profitability.

10. **Case Studies and Success Stories:**
    - Gain inspiration and insights from real-world examples of successful e-commerce businesses, and learn from their experiences and mistakes.

11. **Conclusion:**
    - We'll wrap up with a recap of the key points covered in the book, along with encouragement and actionable next steps to help you on your journey to building a profitable e-commerce business.

Each chapter is packed with detailed information, practical tips, and actionable strategies to help you navigate the complexities of e-commerce and achieve profitability. Whether you're looking to optimize your existing business or start a new venture, this book is your comprehensive guide to e-commerce success.

Chapter One

Getting Started with E-commerce

Choosing the Right E-commerce Platform

Selecting the right e-commerce platform is the foundation of a successful online store. This decision impacts the functionality, scalability, and overall performance of your business. Here are the key factors to consider when choosing an e-commerce platform:

1. **Ease of Use**
    - **User Interface:** Look for a platform with a user-friendly interface that allows you to manage your store without needing extensive technical knowledge.
    - **Setup Process:** The setup process should be straightforward, with clear instructions and support available if needed.
    - **Customization Options:** Ensure the platform offers customization options to tailor the store to your brand's look and feel.

2. **Scalability**
    - **Growth Potential:** Choose a platform that can grow with your business. It should handle increased traffic, sales, and inventory as your business expands.
    - **Upgrading Options:** Check if the platform offers different plans that you can upgrade to as your business needs change.
3. **Payment Options**
    - **Payment Gateways:** The platform should support multiple payment gateways to provide flexibility to your customers. Common options include PayPal, Stripe, and credit card payments.
    - **Transaction Fees:** Be aware of any transaction fees associated with the payment gateways. Some platforms may charge additional fees for certain payment methods.

4. Security
    - **SSL Certificates:** Ensure the platform provides SSL certificates to secure customer data and transactions.
    - **PCI Compliance:** The platform should comply with Payment Card Industry Data Security Standards (PCI DSS) to protect sensitive payment information.
5. SEO Features
    - **Search Engine Optimization (SEO):** The platform should offer SEO tools and features to help your store rank higher in search engine results.
    - **Custom URLs and Meta Tags:** Look for options to customize URLs, meta tags, and descriptions for better search engine visibility.
6. Mobile Responsiveness
    - **Mobile-Friendly Design:** Ensure the platform provides mobile-responsive themes and

templates, as a significant portion of customers shop using mobile devices.

- **Mobile Optimization Tools:** Tools for optimizing the mobile shopping experience, such as mobile-specific checkout processes, can enhance user experience.

7. **Customer Support**
    - **Availability:** Check the availability of customer support, including whether they offer 24/7 support.
    - **Support Channels:** Look for multiple support channels such as live chat, email, and phone support.
    - **Community and Resources:** Access to a community forum and resources like tutorials and guides can be helpful.

Popular e-commerce platforms include Shopify, WooCommerce, BigCommerce, Magento, and Squarespace. Each platform has its unique features, pricing, and target audience. It's important to evaluate these aspects in relation to your business needs.

Setting Up Your Online Store

Once you've chosen the right platform, the next step is setting up your online store. This involves several steps, each crucial for creating a professional and functional e-commerce site.

1. **Register Your Domain Name**
    - **Domain Selection:** Choose a domain name that reflects your brand and is easy to remember. It should be short, simple, and relevant to your business.
    - **Domain Registration:** Register your domain through a domain registrar or directly through your e-commerce platform if they offer domain registration services.
2. **Choose a Theme or Template**
    - **Template Selection:** Select a theme or template that aligns with your brand identity and provides a good user experience.

- **Customization:** Customize the theme to match your brand colors, fonts, and layout preferences. Most platforms offer drag-and-drop editors for easy customization.

3. **Add Products**
    - **Product Listings:** Create detailed product listings with high-quality images, clear descriptions, and accurate pricing.
    - **Categories and Tags:** Organize products into categories and add tags to improve navigation and searchability.
    - **Inventory Management:** Set up inventory management to track stock levels and avoid overselling.

4. **Set Up Payment Gateways**
    - **Payment Integration:** Integrate payment gateways that your platform supports. Ensure the setup process is secure and functional.

- **Test Transactions:** Perform test transactions to ensure the payment process works smoothly before going live.

5. **Configure Shipping Options**
    - **Shipping Rates:** Define shipping rates based on factors like weight, location, and delivery speed.
    - **Shipping Providers:** Integrate with shipping providers for real-time shipping rates and tracking.
    - **Free Shipping:** Consider offering free shipping for certain order values to incentivize purchases.

6. **Set Up Legal and Financial Policies**
    - **Privacy Policy:** Draft a privacy policy outlining how customer data will be collected, used, and protected.
    - **Return and Refund Policy:** Clearly define your return and refund policies to manage customer expectations and reduce disputes.

- **Terms and Conditions:** Create terms and conditions to outline the rules and guidelines for using your website.

7. **Optimize for SEO**
    - **Keyword Research:** Perform keyword research to identify relevant keywords for your products and pages.
    - **On-Page SEO:** Optimize product titles, descriptions, and meta tags with targeted keywords.
    - **Blog Content:** Create blog content to drive organic traffic and establish your store as an authority in your niche.

8. **Test Your Store**
    - **Functionality Testing:** Test all aspects of your store, including navigation, checkout process, payment gateways, and mobile responsiveness.
    - **User Experience:** Ask friends or family to test your store and provide feedback on their shopping experience.

9. **Launch Your Store**
    - **Soft Launch:** Consider a soft launch to test your store with a small audience before going public.
    - **Marketing Campaign:** Plan a marketing campaign to promote your store launch through social media, email marketing, and other channels.

Legal and Financial Considerations

Setting up an e-commerce business involves several legal and financial considerations to ensure compliance and protect your business.

1. **Business Structure**
    - **Sole Proprietorship:** Simple to set up and suitable for small businesses. The owner is personally liable for business debts.
    - **Partnership:** Involves two or more people sharing ownership. Partners are personally liable for business debts.

- **Limited Liability Company (LLC):** Provides limited liability protection and is relatively easy to set up. Owners are not personally liable for business debts.
- **Corporation:** A more complex structure with limited liability protection. Suitable for larger businesses or those seeking outside investment.

2. **Business Registration**
   - **Register Your Business:** Register your business with the appropriate government authorities. This process varies by country and region.
   - **Obtain Licenses and Permits:** Check if you need any specific licenses or permits to operate your e-commerce business legally.

3. **Tax Considerations**
   - **Sales Tax:** Understand your obligations for collecting and remitting sales tax. This varies by location and product type.

- **Income Tax:** Ensure you understand your income tax obligations and set aside funds for tax payments.
- **Tax ID Number:** Obtain a tax identification number (TIN) or employer identification number (EIN) for tax purposes.

4. **Financial Management**
   - **Accounting System:** Set up an accounting system to track income, expenses, and profitability. Consider using accounting software like QuickBooks or Xero.
   - **Bank Account:** Open a separate business bank account to keep personal and business finances separate.
   - **Bookkeeping:** Maintain accurate records of all financial transactions, including sales, expenses, and inventory costs.

5. **Legal Contracts and Agreements**
   - **Supplier Agreements:** Draft clear agreements with suppliers outlining terms of purchase, payment, and delivery.

- **Service Contracts:** If you hire contractors or service providers, ensure you have clear contracts in place outlining their responsibilities and payment terms.
- **Intellectual Property:** Protect your intellectual property, including trademarks, copyrights, and patents, by registering them with the relevant authorities.

6. **Privacy and Data Protection**
    - **GDPR Compliance:** If you operate in the European Union or serve EU customers, ensure compliance with the General Data Protection Regulation (GDPR).
    - **Data Security:** Implement robust data security measures to protect customer information from breaches and cyber-attacks.

7. **Insurance**
    - **Business Insurance:** Consider business insurance to protect against risks such as property damage, liability, and cyber threats.

- **Product Liability Insurance:** If you sell physical products, consider product liability insurance to protect against claims of injury or damage caused by your products.

By carefully considering these legal and financial aspects, you can build a strong foundation for your e-commerce business, ensuring compliance and reducing the risk of legal and financial issues down the line.

Getting started with e-commerce involves several critical steps, from choosing the right platform to setting up your online store and addressing legal and financial considerations. By taking the time to carefully plan and execute each step, you can create a professional and profitable online store. Remember to continuously evaluate and optimize your store to stay competitive and meet the evolving needs of your customers.

Chapter Two

Finding a Profitable Niche

In the competitive world of e-commerce, finding a profitable niche is the cornerstone of your success. A well-chosen niche can help you target a specific audience, reduce competition, and position yourself as an expert in your field. This chapter will guide you through the essential steps to identify and validate a profitable niche for your e-commerce business.

Market Research Techniques

Market research is the foundation of finding a profitable niche. It involves gathering, analyzing, and interpreting information about a market, including information about the target market, competitors, and the overall industry. Here are some effective market research techniques:

1. **Identify Your Interests and Passions**
   Start by considering your own interests, passions, and expertise. Building a business around

something you are passionate about can keep you motivated and engaged. Make a list of topics, hobbies, or industries that you are genuinely interested in. This will help you narrow down potential niches that you might enjoy working in.

2. **Keyword Research**

   Keyword research helps you understand what people are searching for online. Tools like Google Keyword Planner, Ahrefs, and SEMrush can provide insights into search volume, competition, and related keywords. Look for keywords with high search volume and low competition to identify potential niches. Here's a step-by-step approach:

   - **Brainstorm Seed Keywords:** Start with broad terms related to your interests.
   - **Expand Keyword List:** Use keyword research tools to find related keywords and phrases.
   - **Analyze Search Volume and Competition:** Focus on keywords with substantial search volume and manageable competition.

3. **Analyze Google Trends**

    Google Trends allows you to see the popularity of search terms over time. It helps you identify trending topics and seasonal patterns. Use Google Trends to:
    - **Compare Keywords:** See how different keywords perform over time.
    - **Identify Trends:** Spot emerging trends and avoid declining markets.
    - **Understand Seasonality:** Recognize seasonal peaks and valleys to plan your inventory and marketing strategies.

4. **Competitor Analysis**

    Understanding your competition is crucial in determining the viability of a niche. Here's how to conduct a competitor analysis:
    - **Identify Top Competitors:** Use search engines and tools like SimilarWeb to find top competitors in your niche.

- **Analyze Their Websites:** Look at their product offerings, website design, pricing, and customer reviews.
- **Evaluate Their Marketing Strategies:** Examine their SEO, social media presence, and advertising efforts.
- **Identify Gaps:** Look for weaknesses or gaps in their offerings that you can capitalize on.

5. **Social Media Listening**

   Social media platforms are valuable sources of market insights. Monitor conversations on platforms like Facebook, Instagram, Twitter, and LinkedIn to understand what people are talking about, their pain points, and their preferences. Use tools like Hootsuite, BuzzSumo, and Sprout Social for social media listening.

6. **Online Forums and Communities**

   Online forums and communities like Reddit, Quora, and niche-specific forums can provide valuable insights into customer needs and interests. Participate in discussions, ask questions, and pay attention to recurring themes and problems that people are facing.

7. **Customer Surveys and Interviews**

   Direct feedback from potential customers can provide invaluable insights. Use surveys and interviews to gather information about their preferences, pain points, and buying behavior. Tools like SurveyMonkey and Google Forms can help you create and distribute surveys easily.

8. **Analyze Online Marketplaces**

   Online marketplaces like Amazon, eBay, and Etsy can provide a wealth of information about popular products and customer preferences. Look at best-seller lists, customer reviews, and product ratings to identify popular items and understand what customers like and dislike.

Identifying Trends and Demand

Once you have gathered data through market research, the next step is to identify trends and demand within your potential niches. Here's how to do it:

1. **Spotting Emerging Trends**

   Staying ahead of trends can give you a competitive advantage. Use the following methods to identify emerging trends:
   - **Industry Reports:** Read industry reports and publications to stay informed about the latest trends and forecasts.
   - **Social Media and Influencers:** Follow industry influencers and thought leaders on social media to see what they are talking about.
   - **Trend Forecasting Tools:** Use tools like TrendWatching, TrendHunter, and Pinterest Trends to discover new and emerging trends.

2. **Analyzing Search Demand**

   Understanding search demand is crucial to gauge the popularity of a niche. Use keyword research tools to analyze search volume and trends. Look for niches with a growing number of searches over time, indicating increasing demand.

3. **Evaluating Product Demand on Marketplaces**

   Online marketplaces can provide insights into product demand. Look for products with high sales volumes and positive customer reviews. Analyze the competition and identify products with a high demand but relatively low competition.

4. **Understanding Seasonality**

   Some niches experience seasonal fluctuations in demand. Use tools like Google Trends to understand the seasonality of your niche. Plan your inventory and marketing strategies accordingly to capitalize on peak seasons.

5. **Identifying Pain Points and Needs**

   Understanding customer pain points and needs is key to finding a profitable niche. Analyze customer feedback, reviews, and forums to identify common problems and unmet needs. Develop products or services that address these pain points.

Evaluating Competition

Evaluating competition is a critical step in validating your niche. It helps you understand the competitive landscape and identify opportunities to differentiate your business. Here's how to evaluate competition effectively:

1. **Identify Key Competitors**

   Start by identifying your key competitors. Use search engines, online marketplaces, and industry directories to find businesses operating in your potential niche. Make a list of the top competitors to analyze.

2. **Analyze Competitor Websites**

   Visit your competitors' websites and evaluate the following aspects:
   - **Product Range:** What products do they offer? Are there any gaps in their product range that you can fill?

- **Pricing Strategy:** How are their products priced? Can you offer competitive pricing or premium products?
- **Website Design and User Experience:** Is their website user-friendly? What can you do to improve your website's design and user experience?
- **Customer Reviews:** What do customers say about their products and services? Identify common complaints and areas for improvement.

3. **Evaluate Marketing Strategies**

   Understanding your competitors' marketing strategies can provide valuable insights. Analyze the following aspects:
   - **SEO and Content Marketing:** What keywords are they targeting? What type of content do they produce? Use tools like Ahrefs and SEMrush to analyze their SEO efforts.
   - **Social Media Presence:** Which social media platforms do they use? How do they engage

with their audience? Analyze their social media content and engagement levels.
    - **Advertising:** What types of ads do they run? Use tools like AdSpy to analyze their ad campaigns on platforms like Facebook and Instagram.
4. **Assess Customer Service and Support**
   Customer service can be a key differentiator in a competitive market. Evaluate your competitors' customer service by:
    - **Contacting Their Support:** Reach out to their customer support with questions or issues and assess their response time and helpfulness.
    - **Analyzing Customer Feedback:** Look at customer reviews and feedback related to their customer service and support.
5. **Identify Opportunities for Differentiation**
   Based on your analysis, identify opportunities to differentiate your business. Consider the following strategies:

- **Unique Value Proposition:** Develop a unique value proposition that sets you apart from your competitors. Focus on aspects like quality, innovation, customer service, or branding.
- **Product Differentiation:** Offer unique or improved products that address unmet needs or solve common problems in your niche.
- **Brand Positioning:** Position your brand to appeal to a specific segment of the market. Develop a strong brand identity and message that resonates with your target audience.

6. **Monitor Competitors Regularly**

   The competitive landscape is constantly changing. Regularly monitor your competitors to stay informed about their strategies and activities. Use tools like Google Alerts to receive notifications about your competitors' online activities.

Finding a profitable niche is a critical step in building a successful e-commerce business. By conducting thorough market research, identifying trends and demand, and evaluating competition, you can uncover lucrative opportunities and position your business for success. Remember, the key to a profitable niche lies in understanding your target market, offering unique value, and continuously adapting to market changes.

In the next chapter, we will explore the process of product selection and sourcing, providing you with practical tips and strategies to find and manage products that will drive your e-commerce success.

Chapter Three

Product Selection and Sourcing

Selecting and sourcing the right products is crucial to the success of your e-commerce business. This section will cover the criteria for choosing profitable products, sourcing options including manufacturers, wholesalers, and dropshipping, and effective inventory management strategies.

Criteria for Choosing Profitable Products

Choosing the right products to sell online involves a strategic approach. Here are the key criteria to consider:

1. Market Demand
    - **Research Trends**: Use tools like Google Trends, Amazon Best Sellers, and social media platforms to identify trending products. Look for products with a consistent demand rather than those that are seasonal or fads.

- **Keyword Analysis**: Utilize keyword research tools such as Google Keyword Planner, SEMrush, or Ahrefs to determine search volumes for potential products. High search volumes indicate strong interest.
- **Competitor Analysis**: Analyze competitors to understand what products are performing well. Study their product offerings, pricing, and customer reviews to gauge market demand.

2. Profit Margins
    - **Cost of Goods Sold (COGS)**: Calculate the total cost of acquiring a product, including manufacturing, shipping, and handling. Lower COGS allows for higher profit margins.
    - **Selling Price**: Set a competitive selling price that covers your costs and generates profit. Consider the perceived value of the product and the pricing strategies of competitors.
    - **Operating Expenses**: Factor in other operating expenses such as marketing,

packaging, and transaction fees. Ensure that the profit margin is sufficient after all costs are deducted.

3. **Unique Value Proposition (UVP)**
   - **Differentiation**: Choose products that offer unique features or benefits that set them apart from competitors. This could include quality, design, functionality, or sustainability.
   - **Brand Alignment**: Ensure that the product aligns with your brand's values and target audience. A strong UVP can attract loyal customers and enhance brand reputation.

4. **Target Audience**
   - **Demographics**: Identify the demographics of your target audience, such as age, gender, income level, and geographic location. Choose products that appeal to their preferences and needs.
   - **Psychographics**: Understand the lifestyle, interests, and values of your target audience.

This will help you select products that resonate with their behaviors and motivations.

5. **Product Life Cycle**
    - **Longevity**: Opt for products with a longer life cycle to ensure sustained profitability. Avoid products that are likely to become obsolete or face significant technological advancements.
    - **Seasonality**: Be aware of seasonal products and plan your inventory accordingly. Diversifying your product range can help maintain steady sales throughout the year.

6. **Supplier Reliability**
    - **Quality Assurance**: Ensure that suppliers maintain high-quality standards for their products. Request samples and perform quality checks before making bulk purchases.
    - **Consistent Supply**: Choose suppliers who can consistently meet your demand without

delays. A reliable supply chain is essential for maintaining inventory levels and customer satisfaction.
- **Communication**: Establish clear and open communication channels with suppliers. This helps in resolving issues quickly and ensures smooth operations.

Sourcing Products

Sourcing products involves finding and partnering with suppliers who can provide the products you want to sell. There are several options for sourcing products:

1. **Manufacturers**
    - **Direct Manufacturing**: Working directly with manufacturers allows you to produce custom products and control the quality and branding. This option is suitable for unique or proprietary products.
    - **Domestic vs. Overseas**: Consider the advantages and disadvantages of domestic and overseas manufacturing. Domestic

manufacturers offer quicker shipping times and easier communication, while overseas manufacturers often provide lower production costs.
- **Finding Manufacturers**: Use online directories like Alibaba, ThomasNet, and Maker's Row to find reputable manufacturers. Attend trade shows and industry events to establish connections and negotiate terms.

2. **Wholesalers**
   - **Bulk Purchasing**: Wholesalers purchase products in bulk from manufacturers and sell them at a markup. Buying from wholesalers allows you to stock a variety of products without the need for direct manufacturing.
   - **Advantages**: Working with wholesalers provides flexibility, as you can order smaller quantities compared to direct manufacturing. It also allows for faster restocking and less upfront investment.

- **Finding Wholesalers**: Utilize wholesale directories like SaleHoo, Worldwide Brands, and Wholesale Central to find reliable wholesalers. Contact local distributors and attend trade shows to explore options.

3. **Dropshipping**
    - **No Inventory Required**: Dropshipping allows you to sell products without holding inventory. When a customer places an order, the supplier ships the product directly to the customer.
    - **Low Upfront Costs**: Since you don't need to purchase inventory upfront, dropshipping reduces financial risk. It's an ideal option for testing new products and markets.
    - **Choosing Dropshipping Suppliers**: Select reputable dropshipping suppliers through platforms like Oberlo, Spocket, and AliExpress. Ensure they offer reliable shipping and quality products.

- **Considerations**: Be aware of potential drawbacks such as lower profit margins, less control over product quality and shipping times, and increased competition.

Inventory Management

Effective inventory management is essential to ensure that you have the right products in stock to meet customer demand while minimizing costs. Here are key strategies for managing inventory:

1. **Inventory Forecasting**
    - **Demand Planning**: Use historical sales data, market trends, and seasonal patterns to forecast future demand. This helps in making informed decisions about inventory levels.
    - **Sales Trends**: Analyze sales trends to identify popular products and anticipate fluctuations in demand. Adjust your inventory levels based on these insights.

2. **Inventory Tracking**
    - **Inventory Management Software**: Invest in inventory management software to track stock levels, monitor sales, and manage orders. Popular options include TradeGecko, Zoho Inventory, and Cin7.
    - **Barcode Scanning**: Implement barcode scanning to streamline inventory tracking and reduce errors. This helps in accurately updating stock levels in real-time.
3. **Reorder Point Formula**
    - **Calculate Reorder Points**: Determine the reorder point for each product by considering lead time, demand rate, and safety stock. The formula is: Reorder Point=(Lead Time×Demand Rate)+Safety Stock\text{Reorder Point} = (\text{Lead Time} \times \text{Demand Rate}) + \text{Safety Stock}Reorder Point=(Lead Time×Demand Rate)+Safety Stock

- **Lead Time**: The time it takes for a new order to arrive from the supplier.
- **Demand Rate**: The average number of units sold per day.
- **Safety Stock**: Additional stock to account for unexpected demand or supply delays.

4. ABC Analysis
    - **Classify Inventory**: Use ABC analysis to classify inventory into three categories based on their importance:
        - **A Items**: High-value products with low sales volume. Prioritize these for tight inventory control and frequent reordering.
        - **B Items**: Moderate-value products with moderate sales volume. Monitor these regularly and maintain optimal stock levels.
        - **C Items**: Low-value products with high sales volume. Order these in larger quantities but less frequently.

5. **Just-In-Time (JIT) Inventory**
    - **Minimize Stock Levels**: Adopt the JIT inventory method to reduce carrying costs by ordering products only when needed. This approach requires efficient supplier coordination and accurate demand forecasting.
    - **Benefits**: JIT inventory reduces storage costs, minimizes waste, and improves cash flow. However, it requires a reliable supply chain and quick response times.
6. **Safety Stock Management**
    - **Buffer Stock**: Maintain safety stock as a buffer to protect against stockouts and demand variability. Calculate safety stock based on lead time variability and demand fluctuations.
    - **Review Regularly**: Regularly review and adjust safety stock levels based on changing demand patterns and supplier reliability.

7. **Inventory Audits**
    - **Regular Audits**: Conduct regular inventory audits to verify stock levels and identify discrepancies. This helps in maintaining accurate records and preventing stockouts or overstocking.
    - **Cycle Counting**: Implement cycle counting, where a portion of inventory is counted on a rotating schedule. This allows for continuous inventory accuracy without disrupting operations.
8. **Supplier Relationships**
    - **Strong Partnerships**: Build strong relationships with suppliers to ensure reliable and timely deliveries. Communicate regularly to address issues and negotiate favorable terms.
    - **Backup Suppliers**: Have backup suppliers in place to mitigate risks of supply chain

disruptions. This ensures continuity in case of unforeseen circumstances.

9. **Automated Replenishment**
    - **Set Replenishment Rules**: Use inventory management software to set automated replenishment rules based on reorder points and sales trends. This ensures timely restocking and reduces manual effort.
    - **Integration with E-commerce Platform**: Integrate inventory management software with your e-commerce platform to sync stock levels, orders, and sales data in real-time.

10. **Inventory Turnover Ratio**
    - **Calculate Turnover**: Monitor the inventory turnover ratio to assess how quickly products are sold and replaced. The formula is: Inventory Turnover Ratio=Cost of Goods Sold (COGS)Average Inventory\text{Inventory Turnover Ratio} = \frac{\text{Cost of Goods Sold (COGS)}}{\text{Average

$$\text{Inventory Turnover Ratio} = \frac{\text{Cost of Goods Sold (COGS)}}{\text{Average Inventory}}$$

- **Optimize Inventory**: Aim for a higher turnover ratio, indicating efficient inventory management. Adjust your inventory levels and marketing strategies to improve turnover.

Choosing and sourcing the right products, combined with effective inventory management, is fundamental to the success of your e-commerce business. By following the criteria for selecting profitable products, exploring various sourcing options, and implementing robust inventory management strategies, you can ensure that your business remains competitive, responsive to customer demands, and profitable.

Chapter Four

Building a Strong Brand

Building a strong brand is crucial for any e-commerce business aiming for long-term success and profitability. A well-defined brand identity, a unique value proposition, and effective branding strategies can set your business apart from competitors and create lasting connections with your customers. In this section, we will delve into the key elements of building a strong brand, including developing a brand identity, crafting a unique value proposition, and implementing effective branding strategies.

Developing a Brand Identity

1. Understanding Brand Identity

Brand identity encompasses the visual and emotional aspects of your brand that distinguish it from others. It includes elements such as your brand name, logo, color scheme, typography, and overall design. Brand identity is how you present your business to the world and how you want your customers to perceive you.

2. Defining Your Brand

Before you can build a strong brand identity, you need to define what your brand stands for. This involves:

- **Mission Statement:** Your mission statement should clearly articulate the purpose of your business. It answers the question, "Why does my business exist?" A strong mission statement aligns with your business goals and resonates with your target audience.
- **Vision Statement:** Your vision statement outlines the long-term goals and aspirations of your business. It describes what you aim to achieve in the future and serves as a guiding light for your brand.
- **Core Values:** Core values are the principles and beliefs that drive your business. They shape your brand's behavior and decision-making processes.

Clearly defined core values help build trust and loyalty among your customers.

3. Crafting Your Brand's Visual Identity

Your brand's visual identity plays a significant role in how customers perceive your business. Key components include:

- **Brand Name:** Choose a name that is memorable, easy to pronounce, and reflects your business's values and offerings. A strong brand name is unique and stands out in the market.
- **Logo:** Your logo is the visual representation of your brand. It should be simple, versatile, and aligned with your brand's personality. Consider working with a professional designer to create a logo that accurately represents your brand.
- **Color Palette:** Colors evoke emotions and can significantly impact how customers perceive your brand. Select a color palette that aligns with your brand's personality and appeals to your target

audience. Consistency in color usage across all marketing materials is essential.

- **Typography:** The fonts you use in your branding materials should be consistent and reflect your brand's character. Choose fonts that are legible and complement your logo and overall design.

- **Imagery and Graphics:** Use images and graphics that resonate with your brand's message and values. High-quality visuals help create a cohesive and professional brand identity.

4. Developing Your Brand's Voice and Tone

Your brand's voice and tone are the ways you communicate with your audience. They should be consistent across all touchpoints, including your website, social media, and marketing materials. Consider the following:

- **Brand Voice:** Your brand voice reflects your brand's personality and values. It could be formal, informal, friendly, authoritative, or humorous, depending on your target audience and industry.

- **Brand Tone:** The tone of your communication can vary depending on the context. For example, your tone might be more serious in a customer service situation and more casual on social media. Ensure that the tone aligns with your brand voice and resonates with your audience.

5. Establishing Brand Guidelines

Brand guidelines are a set of rules and standards for using your brand elements. They ensure consistency in how your brand is presented across different platforms and materials. Your brand guidelines should include:

- **Logo Usage:** Guidelines on how to use your logo, including size, placement, and variations.
- **Color Palette:** Specifications for using your brand colors, including primary and secondary colors.
- **Typography:** Guidelines for font usage, including font sizes, styles, and spacing.
- **Imagery and Graphics:** Instructions on the types of images and graphics to use, including style and quality.

- **Brand Voice and Tone:** Guidelines for maintaining a consistent voice and tone in your communications.

Creating a Unique Value Proposition

1. What is a Unique Value Proposition?

A unique value proposition (UVP) is a statement that clearly articulates the unique benefits and value your business offers to customers. It answers the question, "Why should customers choose your business over your competitors?" A strong UVP sets you apart in the marketplace and helps attract and retain customers.

2. Identifying Your Target Audience

To create an effective UVP, you need to understand your target audience. Consider the following:

- **Demographics:** Age, gender, income level, education, and occupation.
- **Psychographics:** Interests, values, lifestyle, and behavior.

- **Pain Points:** Challenges and problems your audience faces that your products or services can solve.

3. Analyzing Competitors

Analyze your competitors to identify gaps in the market and opportunities for differentiation. Evaluate their UVPs, strengths, and weaknesses. This will help you position your brand effectively and highlight what makes you unique.

4. Crafting Your UVP

When crafting your UVP, focus on:

- **Benefits:** Clearly articulate the benefits your product or service offers. How does it solve your customers' problems or improve their lives?
- **Differentiation:** Highlight what sets your business apart from competitors. What makes your offering unique or superior?
- **Clarity:** Ensure your UVP is clear, concise, and easy to understand. Avoid jargon and focus on

delivering a message that resonates with your target audience.

5. Testing and Refining Your UVP

Once you've developed your UVP, test it with your target audience. Gather feedback and make adjustments as needed. A strong UVP should evolve with your business and market conditions.

Effective Branding Strategies

1. Building Brand Awareness

Brand awareness is the extent to which customers recognize and recall your brand. Strategies to build brand awareness include:

- **Content Marketing:** Create valuable and relevant content that engages your audience and promotes your brand. This could include blog posts, videos, infographics, and social media content.
- **Social Media Marketing:** Utilize social media platforms to reach and engage with your

audience. Consistent posting, interaction, and advertising can help increase brand visibility.

- **Influencer Marketing:** Partner with influencers who align with your brand values to promote your products or services. Influencers can help reach new audiences and build credibility.
- **Public Relations:** Use PR strategies to gain media coverage and increase brand exposure. This could involve press releases, media interviews, and partnerships with relevant organizations.

2. Enhancing Customer Experience

A positive customer experience can strengthen your brand and build loyalty. Focus on:

- **User-Friendly Website:** Ensure your website is easy to navigate, visually appealing, and optimized for mobile devices. A seamless user experience enhances brand perception.
- **Customer Service:** Provide excellent customer service through multiple channels, including

email, chat, and phone. Prompt and helpful responses can create positive brand associations.

- **Personalization:** Personalize your interactions with customers based on their preferences and behavior. Tailored recommendations and offers can enhance the customer experience.

3. Building Brand Loyalty

Brand loyalty is the commitment customers have towards your brand. Strategies to build loyalty include:

- **Loyalty Programs:** Implement reward programs that incentivize repeat purchases and engagement. Offer discounts, points, or exclusive benefits to loyal customers.
- **Customer Feedback:** Actively seek and act on customer feedback. Show that you value their opinions and make improvements based on their suggestions.
- **Consistent Engagement:** Maintain regular communication with your customers through email newsletters, social media, and other

channels. Keep them informed about new products, promotions, and updates.

4. Leveraging Brand Partnerships

Brand partnerships can enhance your brand's reach and credibility. Consider:

- **Collaborations:** Partner with complementary brands or businesses to create joint marketing campaigns or product offerings.
- **Co-Branding:** Collaborate with another brand to create a co-branded product or service. This can leverage the strengths of both brands and attract new customers.
- **Sponsorships:** Sponsor events, activities, or causes that align with your brand values. This can increase brand visibility and create positive associations.

5. Measuring Brand Performance

Regularly evaluate your brand's performance to ensure it is meeting your goals. Key metrics to track include:

- **Brand Awareness:** Monitor metrics such as website traffic, social media engagement, and media coverage.
- **Customer Satisfaction:** Use surveys and feedback tools to gauge customer satisfaction and identify areas for improvement.
- **Brand Loyalty:** Track metrics related to repeat purchases, customer retention, and loyalty program participation.
- **Sales Performance:** Analyze sales data to assess the impact of your branding efforts on revenue and profitability.

Building a strong brand is a comprehensive process that involves developing a clear brand identity, crafting a unique value proposition, and implementing effective branding strategies. By focusing on these key elements, you can create a brand that stands out in the marketplace, resonates with your target audience, and drives long-term success. Remember that branding is an ongoing effort that requires regular evaluation and adaptation to stay relevant and competitive in the ever-evolving e-commerce landscape.

Chapter Five

Optimizing Your Online Store

Optimizing your online store is crucial to maximizing your e-commerce success. In this chapter, we'll explore how to enhance user experience, improve product presentation, and ensure your site is fully optimized for mobile users. Our goal is to help you create a seamless, engaging shopping experience that drives conversions and boosts your profitability.

1. User-Friendly Website Design

1.1. Importance of User-Friendly Design

User-friendly website design is pivotal in e-commerce because it directly affects the customer experience. A well-designed site not only attracts visitors but also encourages them to stay longer, explore more products, and complete purchases. Key aspects of user-friendly design include ease of navigation, intuitive layouts, and accessibility.

1.2. Key Elements of a User-Friendly Design

- **Navigation:** Clear and logical navigation helps users find what they're looking for quickly. Use a simple menu structure with categories and subcategories that reflect your product range. Implement a search bar with auto-suggestions and filters to facilitate product searches.
- **Layout:** Design your homepage and product pages with a clean and organized layout. Avoid clutter by using ample white space, clear headings, and concise text. Group related items together and place important elements (like call-to-action buttons) where they're easily visible.
- **Loading Speed:** A slow website can frustrate users and lead to higher bounce rates. Optimize your site's loading speed by compressing images, minimizing HTTP requests, and utilizing content delivery networks (CDNs). Tools like Google PageSpeed Insights can help assess and improve your site's performance.

- **Consistency:** Maintain a consistent design throughout your site, including fonts, colors, and button styles. This creates a cohesive look and helps users feel comfortable and familiar with your brand.

1.3. Accessibility Considerations

Ensure your website is accessible to all users, including those with disabilities. Use high-contrast colors for text and backgrounds, provide alt text for images, and implement keyboard navigation. Follow the Web Content Accessibility Guidelines (WCAG) to make your site inclusive.

1.4. User Experience (UX) Design Principles

- **Simplicity:** Keep your design straightforward. Avoid unnecessary features or complex layouts that can confuse users. Focus on delivering a clear and enjoyable shopping experience.
- **Feedback:** Provide visual feedback for user actions, such as adding items to the cart or

completing a purchase. This reassures users that their actions have been successful.

- **Error Handling:** Design clear error messages and guides to help users recover from mistakes, such as incorrect form entries or failed payments.

2. Product Descriptions and Images

2.1. Crafting Effective Product Descriptions

Product descriptions play a crucial role in convincing customers to make a purchase. A well-written description should provide all the information users need to make an informed decision.

- **Clear and Concise:** Write descriptions that are easy to read and understand. Use bullet points for key features and benefits, and keep paragraphs short and focused.
- **Highlight Benefits:** Emphasize the benefits of the product rather than just listing features. Explain how the product solves a problem or improves the customer's life.

- **Include Specifications:** Provide detailed specifications such as size, material, color options, and any other relevant details. This helps users understand exactly what they're buying.
- **Use Keywords:** Incorporate relevant keywords into your descriptions to improve search engine optimization (SEO). This helps your products appear in search results when potential customers are looking for similar items.
- **Tell a Story:** Engage customers by telling a story about the product. This could include its origin, manufacturing process, or how it fits into a lifestyle.

2.2. High-Quality Product Images

Images are a vital component of online shopping, as they allow customers to see the product in detail. High-quality images can significantly impact purchasing decisions.

- **Multiple Angles:** Provide images of the product from different angles to give customers a comprehensive view. Include close-ups of important details and any variations, such as different colors or patterns.
- **Zoom Functionality:** Implement a zoom feature that allows users to examine product details up close. This can help them get a better sense of the product's quality and features.
- **Lifestyle Images:** Include lifestyle images that show the product in use. This helps customers visualize how the product fits into their own lives and can make it more appealing.
- **Consistency:** Ensure all product images are consistent in style and quality. Use the same background, lighting, and resolution for a professional and cohesive look.

2.3. Product Videos

In addition to images, product videos can provide a dynamic view of your products. Videos can demonstrate how the product works, show it in action, or provide additional information that's not easily conveyed through images alone.

- **Demonstrations:** Create videos that demonstrate how to use the product. This can be particularly useful for complex items or those with multiple features.
- **Customer Testimonials:** Incorporate video testimonials from satisfied customers. This can build trust and provide social proof.
- **How-To Guides:** Produce how-to guides or tutorials related to the product. This adds value and can help potential customers make informed decisions.

3. Mobile Optimization

3.1. Importance of Mobile Optimization

With a growing number of consumers shopping on mobile devices, ensuring your online store is mobile-friendly is essential. Mobile optimization improves user experience, enhances accessibility, and can boost conversion rates.

3.2. Responsive Design

Responsive design ensures that your website adjusts seamlessly to different screen sizes and devices. This involves:

- **Fluid Grids:** Use fluid grids that resize content proportionally based on the screen size. This ensures that your site looks good on both large screens and small mobile devices.
- **Flexible Images:** Implement responsive images that scale according to the device's resolution. Use techniques like CSS media queries to adjust image sizes as needed.
- **Viewport Meta Tag:** Use the viewport meta tag to control the layout on mobile browsers. This ensures that your site is displayed correctly on various devices.

3.3. Mobile-Specific Features

- **Touchscreen Navigation:** Optimize navigation for touchscreen devices. Use larger buttons, touch-friendly controls, and avoid hover-dependent features.
- **Mobile Payment Options:** Integrate mobile-friendly payment options such as digital wallets (e.g., Apple Pay, Google Wallet) to streamline the checkout process on mobile devices.
- **Simplified Forms:** Design mobile forms to be easy to complete. Use autofill options, large input fields, and minimize the number of required fields to enhance the user experience.

3.4. Testing and Optimization

Regularly test your site's mobile performance using tools like Google's Mobile-Friendly Test. Analyze user behavior on mobile devices and make adjustments as needed to improve functionality and user experience.

3.5. Page Speed on Mobile

Mobile users often have slower internet connections, so optimizing page speed is crucial.

- **Optimize Images:** Compress images for faster loading times without sacrificing quality.
- **Minimize Code:** Reduce the amount of JavaScript and CSS to improve load times. Use asynchronous loading for non-essential scripts.
- **Enable Caching:** Utilize browser caching to speed up load times for returning visitors.

3.6. User Experience on Mobile

Ensure a seamless mobile experience by focusing on:

- **Readable Text:** Use legible fonts and appropriate font sizes for mobile devices. Avoid requiring users to zoom in to read text.
- **Easy Navigation:** Ensure menus and buttons are easy to tap. Avoid overcrowding the screen with too many elements.

- **Accessible Contact Information:** Make it easy for mobile users to contact you. Include clickable phone numbers and email links.

Optimizing your online store is a multi-faceted process that involves creating a user-friendly design, crafting compelling product descriptions and images, and ensuring mobile compatibility. By focusing on these areas, you can enhance the shopping experience for your customers, drive higher conversion rates, and ultimately increase your e-commerce profitability.

Remember, continuous testing and refinement are key. Stay up-to-date with the latest trends and technologies, and always listen to customer feedback to make ongoing improvements to your online store

Chapter Six

Marketing and Sales Strategies

Effective marketing and sales strategies are critical for the success of any e-commerce business. In this section, we'll explore four key strategies: Search Engine Optimization (SEO), Pay-Per-Click (PPC) Advertising, Social Media Marketing, and Email Marketing. Each strategy will be broken down with comprehensive details to help you understand and implement them effectively.

1. Search Engine Optimization (SEO)

What is SEO?

Search Engine Optimization (SEO) is the process of optimizing your online store so that it ranks higher in search engine results pages (SERPs). Higher rankings lead to more visibility and increased organic traffic to your website. SEO involves both on-page and off-page strategies to improve your website's relevance and authority.

Key Components of SEO

1. **Keyword Research:**
   - **Identifying Keywords:** Use tools like Google Keyword Planner, Ahrefs, or SEMrush to find relevant keywords that potential customers are searching for. Focus on keywords with high search volume and low competition.
   - **Long-Tail Keywords:** Incorporate long-tail keywords (e.g., "best eco-friendly yoga mats") that are more specific and less competitive, which can drive targeted traffic.
2. **On-Page SEO:**
   - **Title Tags and Meta Descriptions:** Write compelling and keyword-rich title tags and meta descriptions for each page. These elements appear in search results and influence click-through rates.

- **URL Structure:** Use clean and descriptive URLs (e.g., `yourstore.com/organic-green-tea`) that include your target keywords.
- **Headings and Content:** Use H1, H2, and H3 tags to structure your content, making it easier for search engines to understand. Ensure your content is relevant, engaging, and optimized with keywords.
- **Images and Alt Text:** Optimize images by compressing them to improve load times and adding descriptive alt text for better search visibility.

3. **Off-Page SEO:**
   - **Backlinks:** Acquire high-quality backlinks from reputable websites. Backlinks signal to search engines that your site is authoritative and trustworthy.
   - **Social Signals:** Social media activity can indirectly influence SEO by increasing visibility and driving traffic. Share content

and engage with your audience to build your brand's online presence.

4. **Technical SEO:**
   - **Site Speed:** Ensure your website loads quickly on both desktop and mobile devices. Use tools like Google PageSpeed Insights to identify and fix speed issues.
   - **Mobile-Friendliness:** Optimize your site for mobile users, as a significant portion of e-commerce traffic comes from mobile devices.
   - **XML Sitemap:** Create and submit an XML sitemap to search engines to help them index your site's pages.

5. **Local SEO:**
   - **Google My Business:** Set up and optimize your Google My Business profile if you have a physical store or serve local customers. Include accurate information, photos, and encourage customer reviews.

- **Local Keywords:** Use location-based keywords to attract local traffic (e.g., "best coffee shop in New York").

Measuring SEO Success

- **Google Analytics:** Track organic traffic, bounce rates, and conversion rates.
- **Google Search Console:** Monitor your website's performance in search results, including keyword rankings and indexing issues.
- **SEO Tools:** Use tools like Moz or Ahrefs to track your site's SEO metrics and make data-driven improvements.

2. Pay-Per-Click (PPC) Advertising

What is PPC Advertising?

Pay-Per-Click (PPC) advertising is a model where you pay a fee each time someone clicks on your ad. PPC is a powerful way to drive targeted traffic to your website quickly and effectively.

Types of PPC Ads

1. **Search Ads:**
    - **Google Ads:** Create ads that appear on Google's search results pages. Bid on keywords relevant to your products or services. Google Ads allows you to target specific demographics, locations, and devices.

2. **Display Ads:**
    - **Google Display Network:** Display visual ads on websites across the internet. These ads can be targeted based on user interests, demographics, and past behavior.

3. **Social Media Ads:**
    - **Facebook Ads:** Utilize Facebook's robust targeting options to reach users based on their interests, behaviors, and demographics.
    - **Instagram Ads:** Leverage visually appealing ads on Instagram to engage with users through images and videos.

4. **Shopping Ads:**
   - **Google Shopping:** Show product listings with images, prices, and store names directly in Google search results. This format is highly effective for e-commerce stores.

Creating Effective PPC Campaigns

1. **Keyword Selection:**
   - **Research and Selection:** Use keyword research tools to find high-performing keywords for your ads. Focus on a mix of broad and long-tail keywords.
2. **Ad Copy:**
   - **Craft Compelling Ads:** Write clear, persuasive ad copy that highlights your unique selling points and includes a strong call-to-action (CTA).
   - **Test and Optimize:** Perform A/B testing on different ad copies to identify what resonates best with your audience.

3. **Landing Pages:**
   - **Optimize for Conversions:** Ensure your landing pages are relevant to your ads and designed to convert visitors into customers. Include clear CTAs, product information, and easy navigation.
4. **Budget and Bidding:**
   - **Set a Budget:** Determine how much you are willing to spend daily or monthly. Monitor your spending to ensure it aligns with your goals.
   - **Bid Strategies:** Choose bidding strategies (e.g., cost-per-click (CPC), cost-per-impression (CPM)) that align with your objectives and adjust as needed based on performance.

Measuring PPC Success

- **Google Ads Dashboard:** Track metrics such as click-through rate (CTR), cost-per-click (CPC), and conversion rate.

- **Conversion Tracking:** Set up conversion tracking to measure the effectiveness of your ads in generating sales or other desired actions.
- **Analytics Tools:** Use Google Analytics and other tools to analyze traffic sources and ROI from your PPC campaigns.

3. Social Media Marketing

What is Social Media Marketing?

Social media marketing involves using social media platforms to promote your products or services, engage with your audience, and drive traffic to your website. It's a crucial part of building your brand and increasing your reach.

Key Social Media Platforms

1. **Facebook:**
    - **Business Page:** Create a business page to share updates, promotions, and engage with your audience.

- **Facebook Ads:** Use targeted ads to reach specific demographics and interests.

2. **Instagram:**
    - **Visual Content:** Post high-quality images and videos showcasing your products. Use Stories and Reels to engage users.
    - **Influencer Marketing:** Collaborate with influencers to promote your products to their followers.

3. **Twitter:**
    - **Real-Time Updates:** Share timely updates, engage in conversations, and respond to customer inquiries.
    - **Hashtags:** Use relevant hashtags to increase the visibility of your tweets.

4. **LinkedIn:**
    - **Professional Networking:** Connect with industry professionals, share content related to your business, and engage in discussions.

5. **Pinterest:**
   - **Visual Discovery:** Pin high-quality images of your products to boards, and use rich pins to provide more information.

Creating a Social Media Strategy

1. **Define Goals:**
   - **Objectives:** Set clear goals for your social media efforts, such as increasing brand awareness, driving website traffic, or boosting sales.
2. **Audience Research:**
   - **Understand Your Audience:** Use analytics tools to understand your audience's preferences, behaviors, and demographics.
3. **Content Creation:**
   - **Engaging Content:** Create a mix of content, including product updates, behind-the-scenes looks, customer testimonials, and educational posts.

- **Content Calendar:** Plan and schedule your content in advance to maintain consistency.

4. **Engagement:**
    - **Interact with Followers:** Respond to comments, messages, and reviews promptly. Engage with your audience by asking questions and encouraging discussions.

5. **Analytics and Optimization:**
    - **Track Performance:** Use platform-specific analytics tools to measure engagement, reach, and other key metrics.
    - **Adjust Strategies:** Analyze the data to identify what works and make necessary adjustments to your strategy.

Measuring Social Media Success

- **Engagement Metrics:** Track likes, shares, comments, and follower growth.
- **Traffic and Conversions:** Use Google Analytics to measure traffic and conversions from social media channels.

- **Campaign Analysis:** Evaluate the performance of specific campaigns and promotions to determine their effectiveness.

4. Email Marketing

What is Email Marketing?

Email marketing involves sending targeted emails to your subscribers to promote products, share updates, and nurture customer relationships. It's a powerful tool for driving repeat business and maintaining customer engagement.

Key Components of Email Marketing

1. **Building an Email List:**
    - **Lead Magnets:** Offer incentives like discounts or free resources to encourage users to subscribe to your email list.
    - **Signup Forms:** Place signup forms on your website, blog, and social media profiles.

2. **Segmenting Your Audience:**
    - **Targeted Campaigns:** Segment your email list based on factors like purchase history, interests, and behavior to send more relevant and personalized content.
3. **Crafting Effective Emails:**
    - **Subject Lines:** Write compelling subject lines that grab attention and encourage opens.
    - **Content:** Provide valuable content, including product updates, promotions, and educational information. Use engaging visuals and clear CTAs.
    - **Personalization:** Use recipient names and personalize content based on their preferences and past interactions.
4. **Automation:**
    - **Email Sequences:** Set up automated email sequences for onboarding new subscribers, abandoned cart reminders, and follow-up emails.

- **Trigger-Based Emails:** Send emails triggered by specific actions, such as a purchase or website visit.

5. **Design and Testing:**
    - **Responsive Design:** Ensure your emails are mobile-friendly and look good on all devices.
    - **A/B Testing:** Test different elements of your emails, such as subject lines, content, and CTAs, to identify what performs best.

Measuring Email Marketing Success

- **Open Rates:** Track the percentage of recipients who open your emails.
- **Click-Through Rates (CTR):** Measure the percentage of recipients who click on links within your emails.
- **Conversion Rates:** Analyze how many email recipients complete a desired action, such as making a purchase.
- **Bounce Rates:** Monitor the percentage of emails that fail to reach recipients' inboxes.

Implementing effective marketing and sales strategies is essential for the success of your e-commerce business. By focusing on SEO, PPC advertising, social media marketing, and email marketing, you can increase your visibility, drive targeted traffic, and ultimately boost your profits. Remember to continually analyze and optimize your strategies based on performance data to stay competitive and achieve long-term success.

Chapter Seven

Customer Acquisition and Retention

Customer acquisition and retention are crucial components of a successful e-commerce business. Attracting new customers and keeping existing ones engaged are key to sustaining profitability and growth. This section explores effective strategies for customer service, building loyalty, and leveraging feedback for continuous improvement.

Effective Customer Service

Customer service is the cornerstone of a positive shopping experience and can significantly impact your business's success. Here's how to excel in customer service:

1. **Provide Multi-Channel Support**
    - **Email Support:** Ensure timely responses to customer queries. Implement automated responses for common questions and provide personalized follow-ups.

- **Live Chat:** Offer real-time assistance on your website. Use chatbots to handle routine inquiries and escalate complex issues to human agents.
- **Phone Support:** For customers who prefer speaking directly, provide a dedicated support line. Ensure your staff is trained to handle various issues effectively.
- **Social Media:** Monitor and respond to customer interactions on platforms like Facebook, Twitter, and Instagram. Social media is often where customers express their satisfaction or frustration.

2. Implement a Knowledge Base
    - **FAQs:** Create a comprehensive FAQ section to address common questions. Update it regularly based on customer inquiries.
    - **Help Guides and Tutorials:** Provide detailed guides and video tutorials on using your products or services. This empowers customers to solve problems independently.

3. Personalize Interactions
    - **Customer Profiles:** Use CRM tools to track customer interactions and preferences. Tailor your responses based on their purchase history and past issues.
    - **Personalized Emails:** Send follow-up emails or offers based on previous purchases. Personalized communication enhances customer satisfaction and loyalty.
4. Train Your Support Team
    - **Product Knowledge:** Ensure your team has in-depth knowledge of your products and services. They should be able to provide accurate information and solve problems efficiently.
    - **Soft Skills:** Train your team in communication skills, empathy, and conflict resolution. Friendly and patient support staff can turn a negative experience into a positive one.

5. **Resolve Issues Promptly**
    - **Response Time:** Aim for quick responses to customer issues. Acknowledge receipt of their concern and provide an estimated resolution time.
    - **Follow-Up:** After resolving an issue, follow up with the customer to ensure they are satisfied with the solution and to prevent recurrence.
6. **Monitor and Improve Service Quality**
    - **Feedback Surveys:** Send surveys to customers after their interaction with support to gauge satisfaction. Use this feedback to identify areas for improvement.
    - **Service Metrics:** Track metrics such as response time, resolution time, and customer satisfaction scores. Analyze these metrics to enhance your service processes.

Building Customer Loyalty

Loyal customers are more likely to make repeat purchases and refer others to your business. Here's how to build and maintain loyalty:

1. **Create a Loyalty Program**
    - **Points-Based Rewards:** Offer points for each purchase, which can be redeemed for discounts or free products. Encourage repeat purchases by making it easy to earn and use points.
    - **Tiered Memberships:** Implement tiers based on spending levels. Provide exclusive benefits to higher tiers, such as early access to sales or special discounts.
    - **Referral Bonuses:** Reward customers for referring new buyers. Offer discounts or free products as incentives for successful referrals.

2. **Offer Personalized Experiences**
    - **Tailored Recommendations:** Use data analytics to provide personalized product recommendations based on browsing and purchase history.
    - **Exclusive Offers:** Send personalized offers and discounts to loyal customers. Show appreciation for their continued support with exclusive deals.
3. **Engage Through Content**
    - **Email Newsletters:** Keep customers informed about new products, promotions, and company news. Personalize content to match their interests.
    - **Social Media:** Engage with customers through regular updates, interactive posts, and behind-the-scenes content. Build a community around your brand.
4. **Provide Exceptional Value**
    - **Quality Products:** Consistently offer high-quality products that meet or exceed

customer expectations. Ensure your products deliver value and solve problems effectively.

- **Excellent Service:** Go beyond resolving issues; strive to delight customers with exceptional service. Small gestures, such as handwritten thank-you notes, can make a big impact.

5. **Build Trust and Transparency**

    - **Honest Communication:** Be transparent about product information, pricing, and policies. Address any issues or mistakes openly and take responsibility.
    - **Customer Reviews:** Encourage customers to leave reviews and showcase positive feedback on your website. Address negative reviews constructively and promptly.

Using Customer Feedback for Improvement

Customer feedback is a valuable source of information for refining your products, services, and overall business strategy. Here's how to effectively use feedback to drive improvements:

1. **Collect Feedback Systematically**
    - **Surveys:** Regularly send surveys to gather customer opinions on various aspects of your business. Include questions about product satisfaction, customer service, and website usability.
    - **Feedback Forms:** Provide easy-to-access feedback forms on your website. Make it simple for customers to share their thoughts and suggestions.
    - **Social Listening:** Monitor social media platforms and online forums for unsolicited feedback. Track mentions of your brand and products to gauge public sentiment.
2. **Analyze Feedback Trends**
    - **Identify Patterns:** Look for recurring themes in customer feedback. Common issues or

suggestions can indicate areas needing improvement.

- **Segment Feedback:** Categorize feedback based on customer demographics or purchase behavior. Tailor improvements to specific segments for more targeted solutions.

3. **Implement Changes Based on Feedback**
    - **Prioritize Issues:** Address the most critical feedback first, especially if it impacts a large number of customers. Develop a plan to resolve these issues promptly.
    - **Communicate Updates:** Inform customers about changes made based on their feedback. Show appreciation for their input and demonstrate that their opinions matter.

4. **Measure the Impact of Changes**
    - **Track Metrics:** Monitor relevant metrics to assess the effectiveness of implemented changes. Evaluate customer satisfaction

scores, sales figures, and other performance indicators.

- **Solicit Follow-Up Feedback:** After making changes, seek additional feedback to ensure that the issues have been resolved and that the improvements meet customer expectations.

5. **Foster a Feedback Culture**

    - **Encourage Continuous Feedback:** Create a culture where customers feel comfortable sharing their opinions. Make it clear that their feedback is valued and contributes to improving the business.
    - **Act on Feedback Regularly:** Regularly review and act on feedback to stay responsive to customer needs and preferences. Demonstrate a commitment to continuous improvement.

Customer acquisition and retention are integral to building a successful e-commerce business. By focusing on effective customer service, building loyalty, and utilizing feedback for improvement, you can create a positive customer experience that drives growth and profitability. Prioritize these areas to foster long-term relationships with your customers and ensure sustained success in the competitive e-commerce landscape.

Chapter Eight

Analyzing and Improving Performance

Key Performance Indicators (KPIs) for E-commerce

1. Sales Metrics

- **Total Sales Revenue:** The total income from sales over a specific period. This metric provides a snapshot of overall business performance and helps in evaluating the effectiveness of marketing strategies.
- **Average Order Value (AOV):** Calculated by dividing total revenue by the number of orders. A higher AOV indicates that customers are purchasing more per transaction, which can be improved through upselling and cross-selling strategies.
- **Conversion Rate:** The percentage of visitors who make a purchase. It's a critical measure of how well your website turns visitors into buyers. A low conversion rate might indicate issues with your site's user experience or product offerings.

2. Customer Metrics

- **Customer Acquisition Cost (CAC):** The cost associated with acquiring a new customer. This includes marketing expenses, sales efforts, and any promotional costs. Lowering CAC while maintaining or increasing revenue is crucial for profitability.
- **Customer Lifetime Value (CLV):** The total revenue you can expect from a customer over their entire relationship with your business. Increasing CLV can be achieved by enhancing customer retention and offering additional products or services.
- **Repeat Purchase Rate:** The percentage of customers who make more than one purchase. High repeat purchase rates are indicative of customer satisfaction and loyalty.

3. Traffic Metrics

- **Website Traffic:** The total number of visitors to your site. Understanding traffic sources (organic search, paid ads, social media) helps in optimizing your marketing strategies.

- **Bounce Rate:** The percentage of visitors who leave your site after viewing only one page. A high bounce rate may suggest that your landing pages are not engaging or relevant to visitors.

- **Session Duration:** The average time visitors spend on your site. Longer sessions typically indicate that users find your content and offerings engaging.

4. Operational Metrics

- **Cart Abandonment Rate:** The percentage of users who add items to their cart but do not complete the purchase. Reducing cart abandonment involves improving the checkout process and addressing potential obstacles.

- **Fulfillment Costs:** Expenses related to order processing, packaging, and shipping. Efficient fulfillment processes can help reduce costs and improve profit margins.

- **Return Rate:** The percentage of products returned by customers. A high return rate might indicate issues with product quality or inaccurate descriptions.

Tools for Analytics and Reporting

To effectively monitor and analyze your e-commerce performance, leveraging the right tools is essential. Here are some key tools that can provide valuable insights:

1. Google Analytics

- **Features:** Tracks website traffic, user behavior, conversion rates, and more. Provides detailed reports on traffic sources, user demographics, and site performance.
- **Benefits:** Offers comprehensive insights into how visitors interact with your site, helping you understand user behavior and identify areas for improvement.

2. Google Search Console

- **Features:** Monitors search performance, indexing status, and potential issues with your site's visibility on Google.
- **Benefits:** Helps you track search queries, monitor backlinks, and identify technical issues that could affect your site's search engine rankings.

3. E-commerce Analytics Platforms

- **Examples:** Shopify Analytics, WooCommerce Analytics, BigCommerce Analytics.
- **Features:** Provides insights specific to e-commerce, such as sales performance, customer behavior, and product metrics.
- **Benefits:** Tailored for online stores, these platforms offer integrated data on sales, inventory, and customer interactions.

4. Heatmap Tools

- **Examples:** Hotjar, Crazy Egg.

- **Features:** Visualizes user interactions with heatmaps, session recordings, and user surveys.
- **Benefits:** Helps you understand how users engage with your site, identify areas of high and low engagement, and optimize user experience.

5. Customer Relationship Management (CRM) Systems

- **Examples:** Salesforce, HubSpot, Zoho CRM.
- **Features:** Manages customer interactions, tracks sales activities, and analyzes customer data.
- **Benefits:** Provides insights into customer behavior, preferences, and interactions, aiding in personalized marketing and improved customer service.

6. A/B Testing Tools

- **Examples:** Optimizely, VWO (Visual Website Optimizer).
- **Features:** Tests different versions of web pages or elements to determine which performs better.

- **Benefits:** Helps optimize website elements such as headlines, images, and calls-to-action based on actual user behavior.

Continuous Improvement Strategies

To ensure sustained growth and profitability, adopting a mindset of continuous improvement is essential. Here are some strategies to help you continuously enhance your e-commerce performance:

1. Regular Performance Reviews

- **Frequency:** Conduct monthly or quarterly reviews of your KPIs and analytics data.
- **Process:** Analyze trends, identify areas of concern, and adjust strategies accordingly. Regular reviews help in staying aligned with business goals and adapting to changes.

2. Implementing Feedback Loops

- **Customer Feedback:** Collect feedback through surveys, reviews, and direct interactions. Use this feedback to identify pain points and areas for improvement.

- **Employee Feedback:** Encourage your team to provide insights on processes and strategies. Their perspectives can offer valuable suggestions for improvement.

3. Data-Driven Decision Making

- **Approach:** Base decisions on data insights rather than intuition. Use analytics to guide strategic choices, such as marketing campaigns, product pricing, and inventory management.
- **Benefits:** Data-driven decisions are more likely to yield positive outcomes and reduce the risk of costly mistakes.

4. Optimizing User Experience (UX)

- **Usability Testing:** Regularly test your site's usability and make improvements based on user feedback.

- **Design Enhancements:** Continuously refine website design, navigation, and functionality to enhance the user experience and reduce friction.

5. Staying Updated with Industry Trends

- **Trends:** Keep abreast of e-commerce trends, emerging technologies, and best practices.
- **Adaptation:** Integrate relevant trends into your business strategy to stay competitive and innovative.

6. Training and Development

- **Team Training:** Invest in training for your team to keep them updated on the latest tools, techniques, and industry knowledge.
- **Skill Enhancement:** Encourage continuous learning and development to improve team performance and capabilities.

7. Testing and Experimentation

- **A/B Testing:** Continuously test different strategies and tactics to determine what works best for your business.
- **Experimentation:** Experiment with new marketing channels, product offerings, and operational processes to find opportunities for growth.

8. Financial Management

- **Cost Control:** Regularly review and optimize your expenses to ensure efficient use of resources.
- **Budgeting:** Develop and adhere to a budget that aligns with your business goals and growth objectives.

9. Building a Culture of Improvement

- **Mindset:** Foster a culture where continuous improvement is valued and encouraged.
- **Innovation:** Encourage creative thinking and problem-solving to drive innovation and enhance business performance.

Analyzing and improving performance is an ongoing process that requires vigilance, adaptability, and a commitment to excellence. By focusing on key performance indicators, utilizing effective analytics tools, and implementing continuous improvement strategies, you can optimize your e-commerce business for greater profitability and success. Remember, the goal is not just to track performance but to actively use the insights gained to drive meaningful changes and achieve sustained growth.

Chapter Nine

Managing Finances and Scaling Up

Managing finances and scaling up are crucial aspects of running a successful e-commerce business. In this chapter, we will delve into effective financial management strategies, explore methods for scaling your business, and discuss how to manage growth and expansion. Whether you're just starting or looking to take your business to the next level, this comprehensive guide will provide you with practical tips and insights.

Financial Management Tips

Effective financial management is the backbone of a profitable e-commerce business. It involves careful planning, monitoring, and control of your financial resources. Here's a detailed look at how you can manage your finances effectively:

1. Create a Budget

A well-structured budget is essential for managing your business finances. It helps you allocate resources efficiently and anticipate financial needs. Follow these steps to create an effective budget:

- **Identify Your Revenue Streams:** Determine all possible sources of income, such as sales revenue, affiliate commissions, and advertising fees.
- **Estimate Expenses:** Include fixed costs (e.g., rent, salaries) and variable costs (e.g., marketing, shipping). Don't forget to account for one-time expenses and seasonal variations.
- **Set Financial Goals:** Establish clear financial goals, such as revenue targets, profit margins, and cost reduction goals.
- **Monitor and Adjust:** Regularly compare your actual expenses and revenue against your budget. Adjust as needed to stay on track.

2. Implement Cash Flow Management

Cash flow management ensures that your business has enough liquidity to meet its obligations and invest in growth. Consider the following practices:

- **Track Cash Flow:** Use accounting software to monitor your cash flow in real-time. This helps you understand when cash is coming in and going out.
- **Maintain a Cash Reserve:** Build a reserve to cover unexpected expenses or slow periods. A good rule of thumb is to have three to six months' worth of operating expenses in reserve.
- **Optimize Receivables:** Accelerate the collection of accounts receivable by offering discounts for early payments and sending regular reminders.
- **Negotiate Payment Terms:** Work with suppliers to extend payment terms or negotiate better terms to improve your cash flow.

3. Monitor Financial Performance

Regularly review your financial statements to assess your business's performance:

- **Profit and Loss Statement:** Analyze your revenue, cost of goods sold (COGS), gross profit, operating expenses, and net profit.
- **Balance Sheet:** Review your assets, liabilities, and equity to understand your financial position.
- **Cash Flow Statement:** Evaluate the cash inflows and outflows from operating, investing, and financing activities.

Use these statements to identify trends, make informed decisions, and plan for the future.

4. Control Costs

Effective cost control can significantly impact your profitability. Implement these strategies:

- **Analyze Cost Structures:** Break down your expenses into categories and identify areas where you can reduce costs.
- **Negotiate with Suppliers:** Regularly review your supplier contracts and negotiate better rates or terms.
- **Use Technology:** Invest in technology that automates processes and reduces manual labor, which can lower operational costs.
- **Outsource Non-Core Activities:** Consider outsourcing tasks like customer service or IT support to reduce overhead costs.

5. Tax Planning

Proper tax planning helps you minimize tax liabilities and avoid penalties. Consider the following:

- **Understand Tax Obligations:** Familiarize yourself with the tax regulations applicable to your business, including sales tax, income tax, and VAT/GST.

- **Keep Accurate Records:** Maintain thorough records of all financial transactions, including invoices, receipts, and bank statements.
- **Consult a Tax Professional:** Work with a tax advisor to optimize your tax strategy and ensure compliance with regulations.

Strategies for Scaling Your Business

Scaling your e-commerce business involves increasing its capacity to handle growth while maintaining or improving efficiency and profitability. Here's how you can effectively scale your business:

1. Automate Processes

Automation can streamline operations and reduce manual effort. Consider automating the following:

- **Order Processing:** Use e-commerce platforms that integrate with inventory and shipping systems to automate order fulfillment.

- **Customer Relationship Management (CRM):** Implement CRM software to manage customer interactions, track leads, and personalize marketing efforts.
- **Marketing Campaigns:** Utilize marketing automation tools to schedule and manage email campaigns, social media posts, and advertising.

2. Expand Your Product Range

Diversifying your product offerings can attract new customers and increase sales. Evaluate these strategies:

- **Conduct Market Research:** Identify gaps in the market and emerging trends that align with your business.
- **Test New Products:** Start with small-scale tests or limited editions to gauge customer interest before fully committing.
- **Partner with Suppliers:** Collaborate with suppliers to offer complementary products or exclusive items.

3. Enhance Your Online Presence

A strong online presence can drive traffic and boost sales. Focus on the following:

- **Improve SEO:** Optimize your website for search engines to increase organic traffic. Use keyword research, on-page SEO, and backlink strategies.
- **Invest in Paid Advertising:** Run targeted ad campaigns on platforms like Google Ads and social media to reach potential customers.
- **Leverage Social Media:** Build a presence on social media platforms to engage with your audience, share content, and drive traffic to your store.

4. Optimize Your Supply Chain

An efficient supply chain ensures that you can meet customer demand and reduce costs. Consider these steps:

- **Evaluate Suppliers:** Regularly assess your suppliers' performance and reliability. Build strong relationships and diversify your supplier base to mitigate risks.

- **Implement Inventory Management:** Use inventory management software to track stock levels, manage reorders, and forecast demand.
- **Streamline Logistics:** Optimize shipping and fulfillment processes to reduce delivery times and costs. Explore options like dropshipping or third-party logistics (3PL) providers.

5. Scale Your Marketing Efforts

As your business grows, your marketing strategies should evolve:

- **Increase Budget:** Allocate more resources to marketing initiatives that are proving successful.
- **Expand Channels:** Explore new marketing channels and platforms to reach a broader audience.
- **Personalize Campaigns:** Use data-driven insights to create personalized marketing messages and offers.

Managing Growth and Expansion

Successfully managing growth and expansion involves maintaining operational efficiency while scaling your business. Here's how to navigate this phase:

1. Plan for Growth

Develop a strategic growth plan that outlines your goals, strategies, and timelines:

- **Set Clear Objectives:** Define specific, measurable goals for growth, such as increasing revenue, expanding into new markets, or launching new products.
- **Create a Roadmap:** Develop a detailed plan with milestones, resource allocation, and timelines.
- **Monitor Progress:** Regularly review your progress against your growth plan and make adjustments as needed.

2. Scale Your Team

As your business grows, you may need to expand your team to manage increased demand:

- **Hire Strategically:** Recruit employees with the skills and experience needed to support your growth. Consider roles in areas like customer service, marketing, and operations.
- **Provide Training:** Invest in training and development to ensure your team can handle new challenges and responsibilities.
- **Foster a Positive Culture:** Build a strong company culture that aligns with your values and encourages collaboration and innovation.

3. Maintain Operational Efficiency

Efficient operations are essential for managing growth:

- **Streamline Processes:** Continuously review and optimize your business processes to improve efficiency and reduce waste.

- **Use Data Analytics:** Leverage data analytics to make informed decisions, identify bottlenecks, and optimize operations.
- **Invest in Technology:** Upgrade your technology stack to support scaling efforts, such as implementing advanced ERP systems or upgrading your e-commerce platform.

4. Manage Customer Expectations

Maintaining high customer satisfaction during growth is crucial:

- **Communicate Clearly:** Keep customers informed about changes, such as new product launches or shipping updates.
- **Maintain Quality:** Ensure that the quality of your products and services remains consistent as you scale.
- **Address Feedback:** Actively seek and address customer feedback to improve your offerings and resolve issues promptly.

5. Prepare for Challenges

Growth can bring challenges, so be prepared to tackle them:

- **Financial Risks:** Monitor cash flow and manage financial risks associated with expansion, such as increased overhead or fluctuating demand.
- **Market Competition:** Stay competitive by continuously improving your offerings and differentiating your brand.
- **Operational Strain:** Address any operational strain by investing in infrastructure, technology, and personnel.

By implementing these financial management tips and scaling strategies, you can effectively manage your e-commerce business's growth and profitability. Remember to continuously evaluate your performance, adapt to changes, and seek opportunities for improvement. With careful planning and execution, you can build a thriving e-commerce business that stands the test of time.

Chapter Ten

Case Studies and Success Stories

In the e-commerce world, understanding real-world examples can offer invaluable insights. This section explores successful e-commerce businesses and the lessons learned from failures. These case studies will illustrate key strategies and pitfalls to avoid, providing a comprehensive guide to building a profitable online store.

1. Case Study: Amazon - The E-commerce Giant

Overview: Amazon, founded by Jeff Bezos in 1994, started as an online bookstore and has evolved into the world's largest e-commerce platform. Amazon's success offers numerous lessons in scalability, customer service, and innovation.

Key Strategies:

- **Customer-Centric Approach:** Amazon's focus on customer satisfaction is central to its strategy. The company introduced innovations like one-click purchasing and personalized recommendations to enhance the shopping experience.

- **Diverse Product Range:** Expanding from books to a vast array of products allowed Amazon to capture a larger market share. Their model of adding new categories based on customer demand is a key strategy for growth.

- **Prime Membership:** Amazon Prime was introduced to enhance customer loyalty and increase sales. The membership offers free shipping, exclusive deals, and access to streaming services, creating a strong value proposition for users.

- **Efficient Supply Chain:** Amazon's sophisticated logistics and supply chain management allow for fast delivery and efficient inventory management. The company's investment in fulfillment centers and technology is critical to maintaining its competitive edge.

Lessons Learned:

- **Customer Experience is Crucial:** Prioritizing customer satisfaction can lead to significant growth and loyalty. Amazon's continuous focus on improving the customer experience has been a major factor in its success.
- **Scalability Matters:** Building a scalable infrastructure is essential for managing rapid growth. Amazon's investment in technology and logistics has enabled it to handle massive volumes of transactions.
- **Innovation Drives Success:** Constantly innovating and expanding product offerings can help capture and retain a broad customer base.

2. Case Study: Warby Parker - Disrupting the Eyewear Industry

Overview: Founded in 2010 by Neil Blumenthal, Andrew Hunt, David Gilboa, and Jeffrey Raider, Warby Parker revolutionized the eyewear industry with its direct-to-consumer model. By offering stylish, affordable eyewear online, the company created a new market niche.

Key Strategies:

- **Direct-to-Consumer Model:** Warby Parker bypassed traditional retail channels, selling eyewear directly to consumers. This approach allowed the company to offer high-quality glasses at a fraction of the cost.

- **Virtual Try-On Technology:** The company introduced a virtual try-on feature on its website, allowing customers to see how glasses would look on their face before purchasing. This innovation enhanced the online shopping experience.

- **Social Impact:** Warby Parker's "Buy a Pair, Give a Pair" program donates a pair of glasses for every pair sold. This social impact initiative not only appeals to customers' sense of purpose but also strengthens brand loyalty.

Lessons Learned:

- **Disrupt Traditional Models:** Challenging established industry norms can lead to significant success. Warby Parker's direct-to-consumer model disrupted the eyewear market and attracted a large customer base.
- **Leverage Technology:** Incorporating technology to enhance the shopping experience can differentiate your brand from competitors. Virtual try-on features provide a valuable tool for online shoppers.
- **Build a Brand with Purpose:** Aligning your business with a social cause can resonate with customers and build a strong brand identity.

3. Case Study: Glossier - Leveraging Social Media for Growth

Overview: Glossier, founded by Emily Weiss in 2014, began as a beauty blog and evolved into a successful e-commerce beauty brand. The company's success is largely attributed to its savvy use of social media and community building.

Key Strategies:

- **Community Engagement:** Glossier built a loyal customer base by engaging with its audience on social media. The brand's focus on user-generated content and customer feedback helped shape its product offerings.

- **Minimalist Product Line:** The company offers a curated selection of beauty products, focusing on quality over quantity. This strategy helps streamline operations and maintain a clear brand message.

- **Direct-to-Consumer Sales:** Like Warby Parker, Glossier sells directly to consumers through its website. This approach allows for better control over the customer experience and higher profit margins.

Lessons Learned:

- **Social Media is a Powerful Tool:** Engaging with customers on social media can drive brand loyalty and provide valuable insights. Building a community around your brand can enhance customer relationships.

- **Focus on Quality and Simplicity:** Offering a curated product line can help establish a strong brand identity and simplify operations.
- **Direct Sales Enhance Control:** Selling directly to consumers allows for better control over the customer experience and can improve profitability.

4. Lessons Learned from E-commerce Failures

Understanding why some e-commerce businesses fail is just as important as studying successes. Here are common pitfalls and lessons learned from failed e-commerce ventures.

1. Overstocking and Inventory Issues:

- **Example:** Many e-commerce businesses have struggled with overstocking, leading to excessive costs and markdowns. Overstocking can tie up capital and lead to waste.

- **Lesson:** Implementing effective inventory management systems and using data analytics to forecast demand can prevent overstocking issues. Utilize just-in-time inventory practices to minimize excess.

2. Poor Customer Service:

- **Example:** Businesses that fail to provide responsive and helpful customer service often struggle with negative reviews and decreased customer retention.
- **Lesson:** Prioritize customer service by offering timely support and resolving issues efficiently. Invest in training for customer service representatives and implement feedback mechanisms.

3. Inadequate Marketing Strategies:

- **Example:** Some e-commerce businesses fail due to ineffective marketing strategies that do not reach or resonate with their target audience.

- **Lesson:** Develop a comprehensive marketing plan that includes SEO, social media, and email marketing. Continuously analyze and adjust strategies based on performance metrics.

4. Neglecting Mobile Optimization:

- **Example:** With the increasing use of mobile devices for online shopping, businesses that neglect mobile optimization often miss out on significant sales opportunities.
- **Lesson:** Ensure that your e-commerce website is mobile-friendly and provides a seamless shopping experience on all devices. Optimize loading times and navigation for mobile users.

5. Failing to Adapt to Market Trends:

- **Example:** E-commerce businesses that do not adapt to changing market trends and consumer preferences can become obsolete.
- **Lesson:** Stay informed about industry trends and be willing to pivot or adapt your business model

as needed. Conduct regular market research to identify emerging opportunities.

6. Poor Website Design and User Experience:

- **Example:** An unappealing or difficult-to-navigate website can deter customers and result in high bounce rates.
- **Lesson:** Invest in a user-friendly website design that enhances the shopping experience. Focus on intuitive navigation, clear product descriptions, and easy checkout processes.

Case studies of successful e-commerce businesses provide valuable insights into strategies that drive profitability, while lessons from failures highlight common pitfalls to avoid. By understanding these examples and implementing best practices, you can build a strong foundation for your e-commerce venture.

Focus on customer satisfaction, leverage technology, and adapt to market trends to position your business for success. With careful planning and execution, you can navigate the challenges of e-commerce and achieve your profitability goals.

Chapter Eleven

Conclusion

Recap of Key Points

As we reach the end of this guide on profitable e-commerce tips, it's essential to reflect on the crucial strategies and concepts we've explored. Building a successful and profitable e-commerce business requires a comprehensive approach, focusing on various facets from choosing the right platform to optimizing your marketing efforts. Here's a summary of the key takeaways:

Choosing the Right E-commerce Platform: Selecting an appropriate e-commerce platform is foundational. We discussed the importance of evaluating different platforms based on your business needs, including ease of use, scalability, customization options, and integration capabilities. Whether you opt for a hosted solution like Shopify or a self-hosted one like WooCommerce, ensuring it aligns with your goals is vital.

1. **Finding a Profitable Niche**: Identifying a niche with high demand and manageable competition is crucial for success. We covered techniques for market research, such as analyzing trends, studying consumer behavior, and assessing competitor strengths and weaknesses. By choosing a niche that resonates with your target audience, you set the stage for a profitable business.
2. **Product Selection and Sourcing**: The selection of products directly impacts profitability. We explored criteria for choosing products, such as profitability margins, demand, and uniqueness. Additionally, sourcing strategies, whether through manufacturers, wholesalers, or dropshipping, play a critical role in ensuring product availability and quality.

3. **Building a Strong Brand**: A strong brand distinguishes your business from competitors and fosters customer loyalty. We discussed the importance of creating a compelling brand identity, including a memorable logo, consistent messaging, and a clear value proposition. Effective branding helps establish trust and recognition in the marketplace.
4. **Optimizing Your Online Store**: Your online store's design and functionality significantly affect user experience and conversion rates. We emphasized the need for a user-friendly design, optimized product pages, and mobile responsiveness. Ensuring a smooth and enjoyable shopping experience encourages customers to complete their purchases and return in the future.

5. **Marketing and Sales Strategies**: Attracting and retaining customers requires effective marketing strategies. We covered various approaches, including SEO to improve search engine rankings, PPC advertising for targeted traffic, social media marketing to engage with your audience, and email marketing for personalized communication. Each strategy contributes to driving traffic and increasing sales.
6. **Customer Acquisition and Retention**: Building a loyal customer base is as important as attracting new customers. We explored techniques for exceptional customer service, such as timely responses and personalized support. Additionally, implementing loyalty programs and leveraging customer feedback helps enhance satisfaction and encourage repeat business.

7. **Analyzing and Improving Performance:** Continuous improvement is key to long-term success. We discussed the importance of tracking key performance indicators (KPIs), using analytics tools to monitor performance, and making data-driven decisions. Regular analysis helps identify strengths, weaknesses, and areas for growth.

8. **Managing Finances and Scaling Up:** Sound financial management and strategic scaling are essential for growth. We covered tips for budgeting, managing cash flow, and reinvesting in your business. As your business grows, planning for expansion and adapting to increased demand are crucial for sustaining profitability.

9. **Case Studies and Success Stories**: Learning from successful e-commerce businesses provides valuable insights. We examined various case studies to understand what contributed to their success and how their strategies can be applied to your own business. Analyzing both successes and failures helps refine your approach and avoid common pitfalls.

Encouragement and Next Steps

As you move forward with your e-commerce journey, keep in mind that building a profitable online business is a dynamic and ongoing process. Here's some encouragement and guidance for the road ahead:

1. **Embrace Continuous Learning**: The e-commerce landscape is ever-evolving, with new technologies, trends, and consumer behaviors emerging regularly. Stay updated by reading industry blogs, attending webinars, and participating in e-commerce forums. Continuous learning helps you adapt to changes and seize new opportunities.
2. **Implement What You've Learned**: Take the insights and strategies from this guide and put them into practice. Start by focusing on one area at a time—whether it's optimizing your website, refining your marketing strategy, or improving customer service. Implementing changes gradually ensures you can manage and measure their impact effectively.

3. **Set Clear Goals and Monitor Progress**: Define specific, measurable goals for your e-commerce business. Whether it's increasing sales by a certain percentage or expanding your product range, having clear objectives helps you stay focused and motivated. Regularly review your progress and adjust your strategies as needed.

4. **Build a Support Network**: Surround yourself with a network of fellow entrepreneurs, mentors, and industry experts. Engaging with others in the e-commerce community provides valuable support, advice, and inspiration. Networking can also lead to partnerships and collaborations that benefit your business.

5. **Be Persistent and Adaptable**: Success in e-commerce doesn't happen overnight. Be prepared for challenges and setbacks along the way. Persistence and adaptability are key traits of successful entrepreneurs. Embrace failures as learning opportunities and stay committed to your vision.

6. **Focus on Customer Experience:** Always prioritize the customer experience. Happy customers are more likely to become repeat buyers and brand advocates. Strive to exceed their expectations through excellent service, high-quality products, and a seamless shopping experience.

7. **Leverage Technology and Tools:** Utilize technology to streamline your operations and enhance efficiency. Tools for inventory management, marketing automation, and analytics can save time and provide valuable insights. Explore and invest in technologies that align with your business goals.

8. **Scale Strategically:** As your business grows, plan your scaling strategies carefully. Expanding too quickly can strain your resources and impact customer satisfaction. Scale at a pace that allows you to maintain quality and manage growth effectively.

9. **Seek Feedback and Iterate**: Regularly seek feedback from customers, employees, and peers. Use this feedback to make informed improvements to your products, services, and processes. Iterating based on feedback helps ensure you're meeting customer needs and staying competitive.
10. **Celebrate Milestones and Successes**: Take time to celebrate your achievements, whether big or small. Recognizing your successes boosts morale and motivates you to continue striving for excellence. Celebrating milestones also reinforces the progress you've made and the goals you've achieved.

In conclusion, creating a profitable e-commerce business requires dedication, strategic planning, and a willingness to adapt and learn. By applying the tips and strategies outlined in this guide, you're well-equipped to navigate the complexities of the e-commerce world and build a successful online store. Embrace the journey with confidence, and remember that each step forward brings you closer to achieving your business goals.

www.ingramcontent.com/pod-product-compliance
Lightning Source LLC
Chambersburg PA
CBHW082235220526
45479CB00005B/1235